STARFISH

Pebble Plus

SEA LIFE

by **Mari Schuh**

CARMARTHENSHIRE COUNTY COUNCIL	
13080067	
Askews & Holts	10-Nov-2015
J593.93	£11.99

raintree
a Capstone company — publishers for children

Raintree is an imprint of Capstone Global Library Limited, a company incorporated in England and Wales having its registered office at 7 Pilgrim Street, London, EC4V 6LB – Registered company number: 6695582

www.raintree.co.uk
myorders@raintree.co.uk

Text © Capstone Global Library Limited 2016
The moral rights of the proprietor have been asserted.

All rights reserved. No part of this publication may be reproduced in any form or by any means (including photocopying or storing it in any medium by electronic means and whether or not transiently or incidentally to some other use of this publication) without the written permission of the copyright owner, except in accordance with the provisions of the Copyright, Designs and Patents Act 1988 or under the terms of a licence issued by the Copyright Licensing Agency, Saffron House, 6–10 Kirby Street, London EC1N 8TS (www.cla.co.uk). Applications for the copyright owner's written permission should be addressed to the publisher.

Editorial Credits
Elizabeth R. Johnson, editor; Aruna Rangarajan, designer;
Kelly Garvin, media researcher; Tori Abraham, production specialist

ISBN 978 1 4747 0480 9
19 18 17 16 15
10 9 8 7 6 5 4 3 2 1

British Library Cataloguing in Publication Data
A full catalogue record for this book is available from the British Library.

Photo Credits
Newscom/Gordon MacSkimming/PictureNature/Photoshot, 19; SeaPics.com: Andrew J. Martinez, 17, Celeste Fowler, 11, Doug Perrine, 15, Tim Hellier, 21; Shutterstock: Andrea Izzotti, cover, 9, 13, Godruma, cover (background), Longjourneys, 7, Vilainecrevette, 5

Design Elements: Shutterstock: Kasia, SusIO, Vectomart

Every effort has been made to contact copyright holders of material reproduced in this book. Any omissions will be rectified in subsequent printings if notice is given to the publisher.

All the Internet addresses (URLs) given in this book were valid at the time of going to press. However, due to the dynamic nature of the Internet, some addresses may have changed, or sites may have changed or ceased to exist since publication. While the author and publisher regret any inconvenience this may cause readers, no responsibility for any such changes can be accepted by either the author or the publisher.

Printed in China

Contents

Life in the sea 4
Up close 8
Finding food 16
Life cycle 18

Glossary 22
Read more 23
Websites 23
Index 24

Life in the sea

Starfish crawl on the seabed.
These colourful animals look
for food to eat.

5

Starfish live in seas and oceans around the world. There are about 1,500 types of starfish. They are found in both shallow and deep water.

7

Up close

Most starfish have five arms.
Some have 40 arms!
If a starfish loses an arm,
it can grow a new one.

9

Starfish can be many sizes.
Some are less than
2.5 centimetres wide.
Others grow to be more
than 1 metre wide.

11

Starfish have tough skin on their thick arms. Short spines protect starfish from predators.

13

Starfish have hundreds of tiny tube feet. Their feet help them to crawl on coral reefs and rocky shores. Their feet grab prey, too.

15

Finding food

Starfish open clam shells with their feet. They push their stomachs outside their bodies. They stick their stomachs inside the clam shells. Then starfish eat their prey.

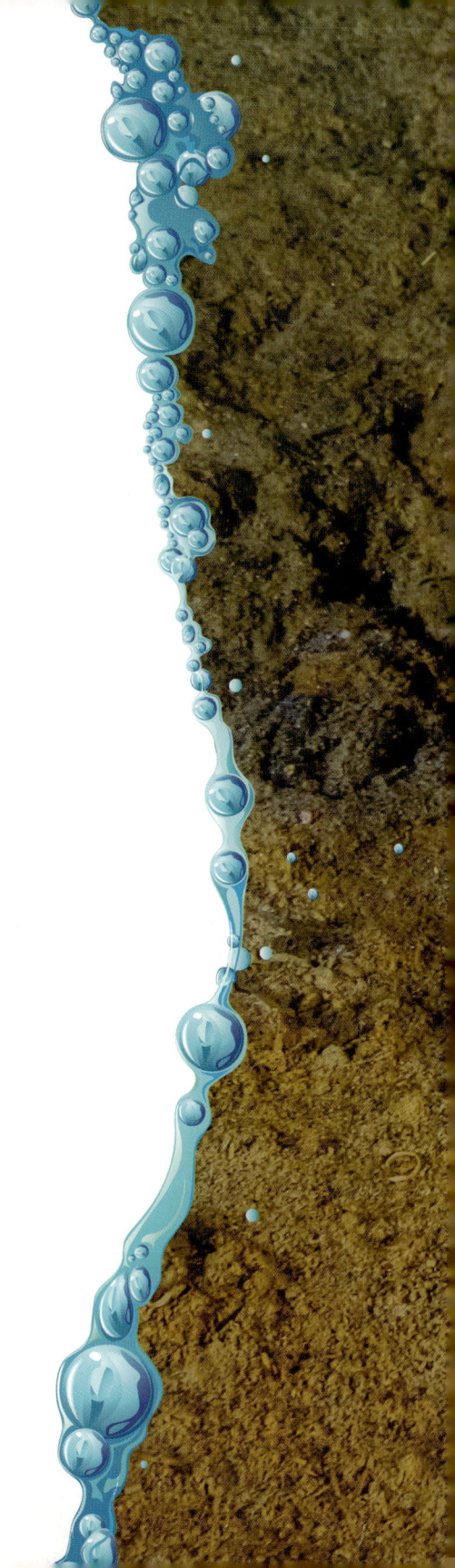

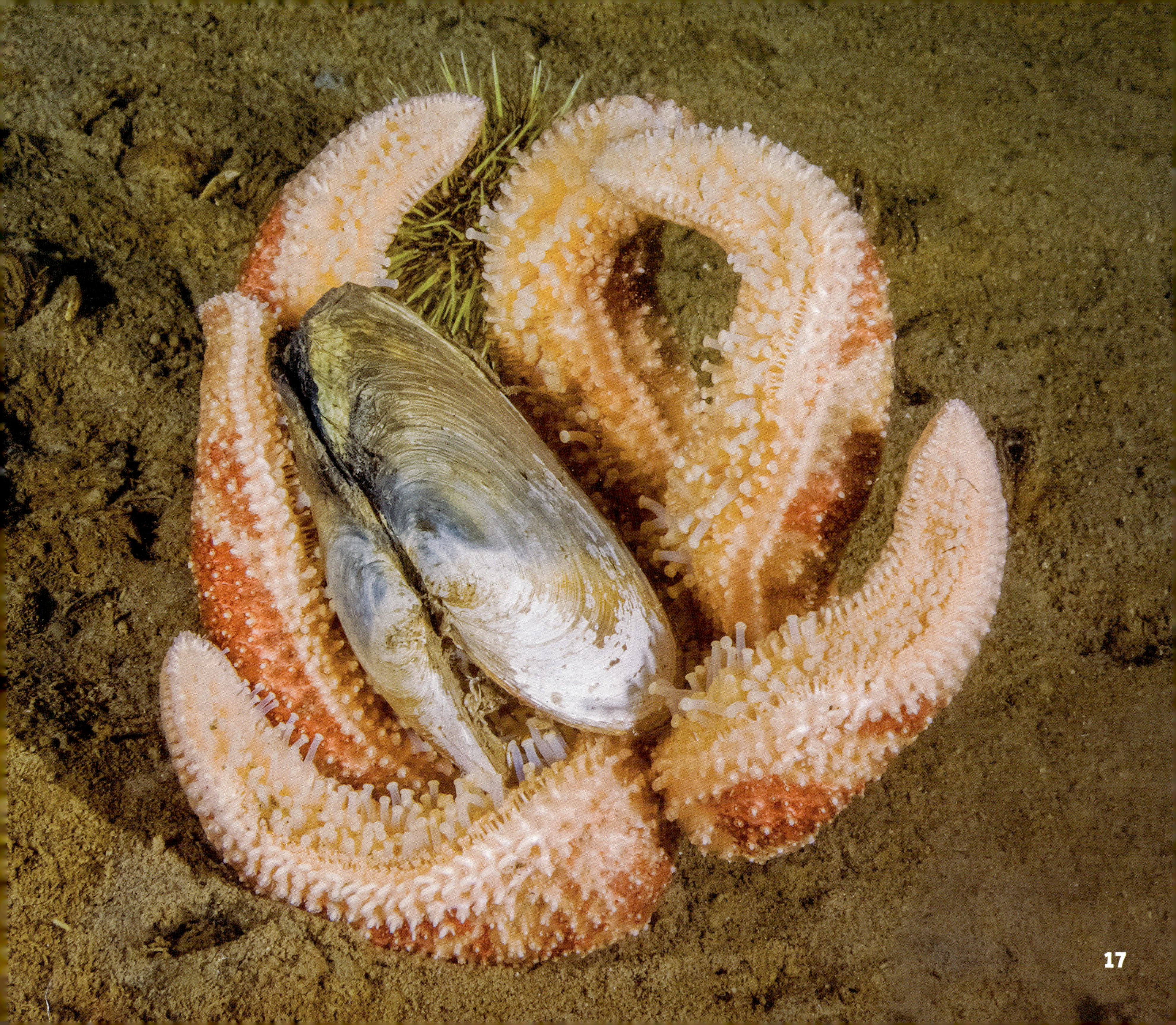

Life cycle

Some female starfish
lay thousands of eggs.
Male starfish put sperm into
the water. When the eggs
and sperm meet,
the eggs are fertilized.

19

The fertilized eggs grow into tiny larvae.
The larvae float in the sea for up to 45 days.
Then they grow into starfish on the seabed.

21

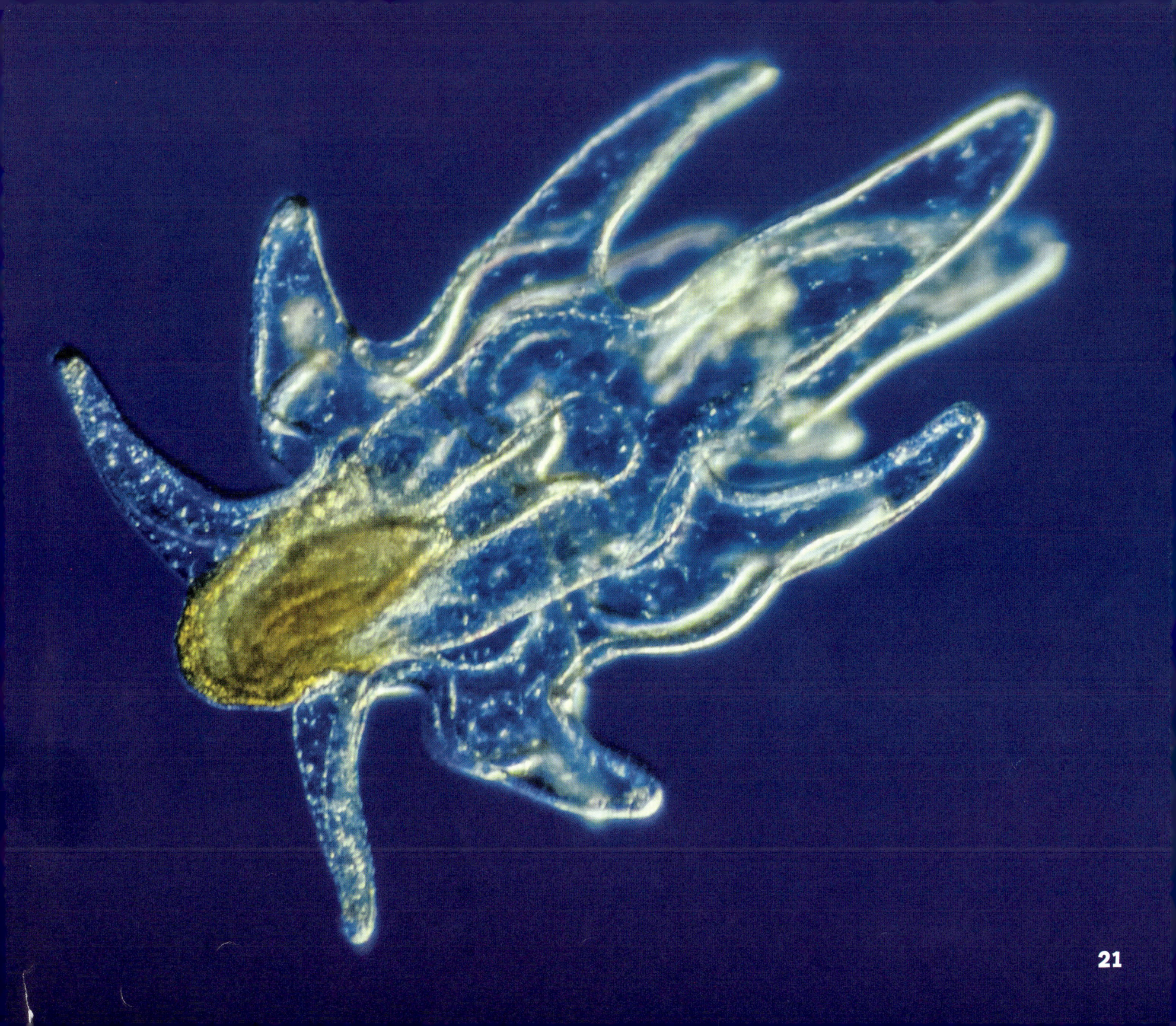

Glossary

coral reef type of land close to the surface of the sea made up of the hardened bodies of corals; corals are small, colourful sea creatures

fertilize join an egg of a female with a sperm of a male to produce young

larva animal at the stage of development between an egg and an adult; more than one larva are larvae

predator animal that hunts other animals for food

prey animal hunted by another animal for food

protect guard or keep something safe from harm

shallow not deep

sperm one of the reproductive cells from a male that can fertilize the eggs of a female

spine hard, sharp, pointed growth on an animal's body

Read more

Fish Body Parts (Animal Body Parts), Clare Lewis (Raintree, 2015)

Sea Animals (Animals in their Habitats), Sian Smith (Raintree, 2014)

Usborne First Encyclopedia of Seas and Oceans, Jane Chisholm (Usborne Publishing, 2011)

Websites

www.bbc.co.uk/nature/life/Sunflower_starfish
Find out about the sunflower starfish.

www.national-aquarium.co.uk/50-fun-facts
Fun facts about sea and ocean life.

Index

arms 8, 12
coral reefs 14
eggs 18, 20
feet 14, 16
food 4, 16
habitat 4, 6, 14

larvae 20
predators 12
size 10
sperm 18
spines 12
types 6